A New Day
Peacemaking Stories and Activities

Carolyn Pogue

Program Ideas for Leaders of Children

A New Day
Peacemaking Stories and Activities for Children
Carolyn Pogue

Copyright © 2005
The United Church of Canada

The stories included in *A New Day* were previously published by Playing for Life, © Carolyn Pogue 2003, ISBN 0-9733284-0-1 with the title *Stories for a New Day*. For permission to reproduce the stories, contact Playing for Life 132 Scarboro Avenue S.W., Calgary, Alberta T3C 2H1.

All rights reserved. No part of this book may be photocopied, reproduced, stored in a retrieval system, or transmitted in any form or by any means, electronic, mechanical, or otherwise, without the written permission of The United Church of Canada.

Exceptions: Full page story illustrations may be photocopied by children's leaders for children to colour. Activities may also be photocopied to enable children's participation.

All biblical quotations, unless otherwise noted, are from the *New Revised Standard Version Bible*, copyright © 1989, by the Division of Christian Education of the National Council of the Churches of Christ in the United States of America. Used by permission.

Care has been taken to trace ownership of copyright material contained in this text. The publisher will gratefully accept any information that will enable it to rectify any reference or credit in subsequent printings.

Library and Archives Canada Cataloguing in Publication

Pogue, Carolyn, 1948-
  A new day : peacemaking stories and activities / Carolyn Pogue.

ISBN 1-55134-139-5

  1. Peace—Study and teaching. 2. Children and peace. I. Title.

JZ5534.P63 2004   303.6'6'071   C2004-906830-X

United Church Publishing House
3250 Bloor St. West, Suite 300
Toronto, ON
Canada M8X 2Y4
416-231-5931
www.united-church.ca/ucph
e-mail: bookpub@united-church.ca

Design: Diane Renault, Graphics and Print
Illustrations: Danka Gocova (front cover and story illustrator)
Lisa Rebnord (activity illustrator)

Printed in Canada

5   4   3   2   1   08   07   06   05   04

Thank You

Thank you to Melinda Lang and Mela Becker for reading the original manuscript.

Thank you to Stewart Duncan and Anne Davies for a peaceful space to write.

Thank you to the children at One World Child Development Centre and at Scarboro United Church in Calgary for inspiration, hope, laughter, and wisdom.

Thank you to Bill, my fellow traveller.

This book is dedicated to the millions of children, teens, women, and men who make peace every day.

Carolyn Pogue

About the Author

Carolyn Pogue of Calgary, Alberta, Canada writes a variety of books, articles, and stories for adults and for children. She is a workshop presenter for all ages and especially enjoys presenting at YouthWrite, a summer camp in the Rocky Mountains for writers aged 12 to 18. "Writing for (a) Change" is one workshop she created to empower writers to use words to change the world.

Carolyn contributes to magazines such as *Canadian Living* and *The United Church Observer*. She has contributed to anthologies such as *Beginnings: Stories of Canada's Past* (Ronsdale Press), and is the author of five books, including *A Creation Story* (Toronto: ParseNip Press/United Church Publishing House) for children and *Language of the Heart: Rituals, Stories, and Information about Death* (Kelowna, B.C.: Northstone Publishing).

Carolyn is a founding member of Women in Black, Calgary. She and her husband, Bill Phipps, share a passion for peace with justice for all creatures great and small. Carolyn is pictured here in the Children's Peace Garden of St. John the Divine Church in New York City.

About the Artist

Danka Gocova was born in Slovakia. After finishing her studies at the Faculty of Architecture of the Slovak University of Technology in Bratislava, she worked as an architect preservationist and was a team member in the architectural council of her hometown of Michalovce. Later, in her own business in Slovakia, she devoted most of her time to creating sacred architecture, art, and illustrations.

Danka, her husband, and their three children moved to Canada in 2001. She now lives in Kitchener, Ontario.

Danka works in a variety of media, including drawing, painting, and glass painting. She illustrates books and creates sacred art for churches.

Contents

Introduction 7
    Create a Peaceful Environment 7
    Include All 7
    Practise Peaceful Problem-Solving 8

"Enough" 11
    Peacing It Together with Today 14
        The Fridge Quiz 14
        Water Tic Tac Toe 15
    Peacing It Together with Our Faith 15
        Thanksgiving Prayer 15
        Peace Passage 16
    Crafting Peace: Solar Power! 16
    Into the World: The Great Canadian Shoreline Cleanup 17
    Activity Page: Water Tic Tac Toe 18–19

"The Egg" 21
    Peacing It Together with Today 23
        Crossword: instructions 23
    Peacing It Together with Our Faith 24
    Crafting Peace: Raise a Flag for the World! 24
    Into the World: Egg Gifts 25
        Saying "Peace" Around the World 26
    Activity Page: Crossword 27

"The Other Flood" 29
    Peacing It Together with Today 32
        Public Speaking 33
        Word Find 33
    Peacing It Together with Our Faith 33
    Crafting Peace: Make Paper and Save a Tree! 34
    Into the World: Working for Equality 35
    Activity Page: Word Find 36–37

"Dragons" 39
Peacing It Together with Today 43
- Anti-Bullying Pledge 44
- Word Play 45
- Dragon Drama 46

Peacing It Together with Our Faith 47
Crafting Peace: War Toys into Art 47
Into the World: Questioning Violence in Media 48
- Ten-Day TV-Free Challenge 49

"The Wall" 51
Peacing It Together with Today 55
- "Peacemobile" Brainstorming 55

Peacing It Together with Our Faith 55
Crafting Peace: Kites of Peace 56
- Peace Words: instructions 57
- Origami Peacemaker: instructions 58

Into the World: Peace Poles 59
- If the Earth - a poem 60
- Peacemakers Everywhere 61

Activity Page: Peace Words 62
Activity Page: Origami Peacemaker 63

Author's Notes 64

Introduction

Peace I leave with you; my peace I give to you. I do not give to you as the world gives. Do not let your hearts be troubled, and do not let them be afraid.

(John 14:27)

Jesus' farewell to his disciples included this promise of peace. Yet in today's world, it is often difficult for children to see and experience peace, and they may even wonder why the world is so violent when we assure them that our Creator is a God of peace. To help the leaders of children in their efforts to "teach peace" against a backdrop of wars played out in the media, bullying in the playground, and greed in our society, Carolyn Pogue has written five beautiful and unique stories. Each story is followed by a range of activities in which the children play out the message of the story and extend its learnings into their everyday lives.

As you engage with children in the peacemaking stories and activities, remember to encourage and lift up all the ways in which the group experience might be leading to the development of peacemaking skills among the participants.

Create a Peaceful Environment

Select and organize your story and activity space so that the concept of peacemaking is given prominence and its message reflected in the atmosphere. Consider playing peaceful, calming music to set the mood for when the children arrive. Avoid rows of furniture. Rather, create space and "air" and opt if possible for floor cushions or other types of soft furnishings. Hang posters or decorate a bulletin board with symbols of peace (check the Internet for a wide range of peace symbol ideas) and/or 'paper' the walls with the word "peace" in many languages (see the illustration on page 20 and the list on page 26).

Create a "peace place" in the room. It could be a table where participants can work out differences they might have with one another. It might also be a soothing space where children can reflect, calm themselves, and cool down.

Include All

One way to avoid conflict in everyday situations is to reduce the potential hurt feelings that come from people being excluded. Welcome each child as they arrive. In situations where the children might not know every participant, arrange for an icebreaker. If you have 'papered' the walls with the word "peace" written in different languages, arrange the children in pairs and suggest that they work together to try and figure out what the languages are.

Other ways to make sure participants feel valued is to include everyone in presentations or group projects, to explain the group's work so that everyone can understand, and to repeat the explanation ensuring that everyone comprehends the project and is ready to participate.

During gatherings, Aboriginal people(s) often use a Talking Stick as a means of ensuring just and impartial communication. According to Aboriginal traditions, the one who holds the Talking Stick has the power of words. Only s/he can speak while holding the stick; other members of the circle must remain silent and listen respectfully. The speaker should not forget that the Talking Stick is sacred. If s/he cannot honour the Talking Stick with the words being spoken, s/he refrains from speaking. Similarly, allow participants in your gatherings to choose an object of peace–it might be a stone or something of particular relevance to your circle of children–to pass during your group discussions, giving everyone a chance to say something. Further guidelines might be that no putdowns or judgments are allowed and that every idea or suggestion will be affirmed before decisions are made. Also reassure the participants that it is not compulsory to say anything. (Peace begins inside each of us, and causing unnecessary stress in the heart of a shy or uncommunicative child would not contribute to a peaceful process.)

At the end of each session, compliment the participants, noting the times you were aware of participants practising peacemaking. Perhaps the children would enjoy being named, in turn, as "peacemaker of the day."

Practise Peaceful Problem-Solving

Describe peaceful methods for problem-solving and use them if conflicts arise within the group. There is a simple process for solving conflict:
- Name the problem.
- Name possible solutions (accept any suggestions even if they are not peaceful).
- Describe the consequences of each solution offered. (Will this solution promote peace?)
- Choose a solution.
- Agree to try again if the chosen solution does not work.

Photocopying
Many of the activities included in this book have been laid out for easy photocopying. The artist, Danka Gocova, also encourages you to photocopy the illustrations for children to colour and post. The illustrations should not be reproduced for any other purpose.

If there is a problem within the group, be sure that you, as the group leader, remain calm as you assist the children in working through the process. It may be necessary to allow time for those in conflict to cool down before beginning the process.

Perhaps your group would also like to develop a prayer of peace that can be spoken at times of conflict or exclusion.

The God of peace be with all of you. Amen. (Romans 15:33)

Amy Crawford
Children's Ministry Staff
The United Church of Canada

Enough • *A New Day*

Enough

Mother Earth was having rather a bad century. She had backaches and migraines like she'd never had before. Father Sky gave her massages and brewed chamomile tea, but the truth is, he wasn't feeling very well either. He'd had a chronic cough for several decades that made him quite tired.

"The thing is," said Mother Earth, "I can't seem to find peace anywhere these days." She would just start making a spectacular sunset, the kind with gold streaks and pink and purple splashed around the edges, and something would happen, like fighting in Africa or America, Asia or Europe. Or she'd just be working on a beautiful design for ice crystals on a frosty morning, and there would be an explosion at a factory, a dam would break, or maybe a ship would leak oil into the ocean.

Mother Earth could find fewer and fewer places to rest and rejuvenate. The days were hard enough, but these years, she wasn't sleeping well either. She lay awake worrying about human violence. She worried about having enough clean space for animals and fish to live. She worried about Father Sky's cough. And she wondered about her own health. There were clogged arteries now where clean, life-giving rivers had once flowed wild and free. There were deep, lifeless craters on her skin where once deer had grazed in meadows of sweet clover.

One crisp autumn morning, Mother Earth was painting maple leaves red, gold, and yellow. There were a lot of leaves to paint and even though they were damaged from acid rain and smog, it was still possible to make them look beautiful. "I'd give anything to get a good night's sleep," she sighed. "Me, too," yawned Father Sky. "People seem all mixed up these days. Their noise kept me awake half the night."

Mother Earth dipped her brush in the gold and carefully edged a leaf. Creating beauty usually helped her think better. "There's so much noise and confusion," she said. "Why are they fighting all the time?"

Father Sky couldn't answer because he suddenly got one of those coughing fits he gets lately. It took a long time for him to get his breath.

"I don't know," he said finally. "We don't seem to be getting through to them anymore." He picked up a paintbrush to help.

Suddenly, there was a tremendous shaking and a thunderous noise. Bluebirds and butterflies shot

11

A New Day
Enough

out of the trees in alarm. At once, an army of huge machines spewing black smoke roared into the forest. They drove over junipers, strawberry plants, and buttercups, and cut down every single tree in their path. Mice and bears, ants and antelopes fled in terror.

A tear rolled down Mother Earth's face. And then another as she watched. "Clear cut," Father Sky said, "so people can get more money." Mother Earth said, "I know. It's like when they mine, when they drill, when they bomb, when they make *progress*." She fell silent; there were no more words to say.

That night when Mother Earth and Father Sky slept, they travelled into Dream Time together. They flew across the star-lit sky and eventually arrived at Moon's place.

"Welcome!" said Moon. "It's been a long time since we visited."

"Too long," rumbled Father Sky.

The three old friends sat for a while in the deep quiet of space, drinking tea and reminiscing about the olden days when the only things in the sky were planets, stars, and dancing Northern Lights. Moon asked, "What's happening down there with the humans? You two look tired."

"We're worried," said Father Sky. "The humans fight and hoard. They seem afraid. They make Mother Earth ache."

"That's serious," said Moon. "Why would they do that?"

"It seems they've forgotten us," said Mother Earth sadly.

"Do you think they've forgotten about Enough?" Moon asked.

"Maybe. We'd always hoped that sunrises would remind them," Mother Earth said, "but these days, humans sit in fast cars and stare at pavement. They don't bother with a sunrise much anymore."

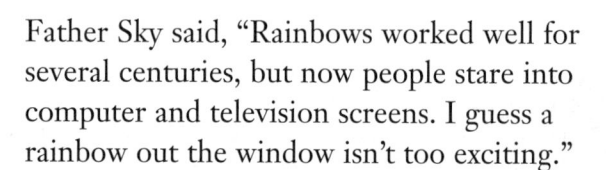

Father Sky said, "Rainbows worked well for several centuries, but now people stare into computer and television screens. I guess a rainbow out the window isn't too exciting."

Moon looked thoughtful. "So all the people everywhere have forgotten about Enough? They don't remember that there is enough light and dark, enough food and water, enough air to breathe? Have they all forgotten?"

For a moment there was a deep silence in the universe. "Well," said Father Sky, "maybe not everyone, exactly. There's Severn. She started The Environmental Children's Organization. And Craig started Kids Can Free the Children. They know about Enough."

"Well, that's a beginning. Are they the only ones?" Moon asked.

"Aha!" said Mother Earth brightening, "Remember Kids for Peace? They're on our side." Father Sky smiled suddenly. "There's UNICEF. And Roots and Shoots!" Mother Earth was wide awake now. "Remember Puppets for Peace? And the Raging Grannies?"

And so, the whole night, Moon listened while Father Sky and Mother Earth named all the children and adults who remember about Enough. While they talked, Moon poured tea and listened to amazing tales of love and friendship, and of

A New Day
Enough

people saving whales and bears, and working for peace even in the scary places.

Suddenly a glimmer of light cracked the sky. "We've talked all night!" cried Mother Earth. "It's time to wake up!"

"Sure glad you dropped up," said Moon. "Thanks for a new perspective," said Father Sky waving. "Goodbye, old friend!"

The next morning, Father Sky gazed at a sparkling blue lake ringed with deep green pines. He looked at golden wheat fields and yellow sunflowers. "Mother Earth," he said, "You are the most beautiful woman in the universe!" Mother Earth's laugh danced on the breeze. "Are you trying to get on my good side?"

"Of course!" he answered. "Then tell me a good story, old man. Tell the story about Enough. Whisper it gently through the trees, so the humans will hear and remember, too." So Father Sky, bending low and speaking gently, began.

"In the beginning, I fell wildly in love with Mother Earth, and she fell wildly in love with me."

"Don't leave out anything," Mother Earth said, closing her eyes and leaning back.

"We came together in Love," Father Sky went on, "and in our Love, we created insects, fish, birds, four-legged and two-legged animals. Life was good. There was enough for everyone. Enough grass and grain. Enough water. Enough animals and fish. Enough land and air. Harmony.

"In the beginning the human animals remembered that there was enough of everything. When humans remember that there is enough, they are happy. They have courage for hard times. They have love for each other and for the planet. It is enough."

Peacing It Together with Today

Canadian activist, Severn Cullis-Suzuki, started to help change the world when she was young. At age 9, she started an environmental group with her friends. At age 13, she made a speech to the first United Nations Earth Summit in Rio de Janeiro, Brazil. Her speech helped shape the *United Nations Earth Charter*. At age 14, she became the published author of *Tell the World: A Young Environmentalist Speaks Out.* Ten years later (with a university degree in evolutionary biology and ecology), Severn is giving speeches all over the world. Her message is clear: Reconnect with the Earth! Find out what you're really eating!

The Fridge Quiz

Share Severn's message with participants: Find out what you're really eating! To discover how advances in science, technology, and rapid transportation are not always used to our best advantage, invite the children to explore what lurks in the kitchen! If there is a refrigerator or other food storage in (or near) your meeting place, invite the children to check the labels on every item of food and drink.

Suggest that they also do their families a favour: Clean out the refrigerator at home and, before putting everything back, check the labels.

Encourage the children to answer the questions below and to share their findings with the group. (If the plan is to check food sources at home, the sharing can take place at a later session.)

1. Where was the food grown?
2. From where was the food shipped?
3. Can all the words on the label be pronounced/understood?
4. Are the fresh products from your own community? Your own country?
5. Which of the products are organic, and which may have been sprayed with pesticides?
6. Is there a possibility of growing food in your yard or house? (Do you already have a garden/allotment?)
7. Discuss your findings with your family members. What surprised you? What surprised them?

Water Tic Tac Toe (see Reproducible Activity Page, page 19)

Invite the children to play water Tic Tac Toe. Directions are on page 18.

Peacing It Together with Our Faith

Thanksgiving Prayer (for any time of the year)

Copy this prayer or, if they prefer, participants might write their own prayers, either as a group or individually. Suggest that the participants take a copy of the prayer home where it can be displayed for everyone in the home to share–perhaps on the door of the fridge.

Creator,

Thank you for *Water* that flows from our eyes when we cry or laugh hard.

Thank you for *Air* coming in and going out of our bodies, miraculously exchanging oxygen for carbon dioxide.

Thank you for *Trusting* us to care for our beautiful planet.

Thank you for *Earth* where we can grow enough food for each person, animal, and insect to live.

Thank you for *Rivers* that give us life, connect cities and towns, and so connect us to each other.

Amen.

Peace Passage

For you shall go out in joy, and be led back in peace; the mountains and the hills before you shall burst into song, and all the trees of the field shall clap their hands.

(Isaiah 55:12)

Nature will celebrate as God's people return to peaceful living in the land God has given to them.

- Invite the children to name ways that they have seen nature celebrate living in peace with humanity. (e.g. a stretch of replanted forest)
- How might nature grieve when humanity harms or destroys it? (e.g. lakes obliterated of all life as the consequence of acid rain)

Crafting Peace: Solar Power!

Create a solar oven as a group project. A solar oven traps the heat of the sun in a box and cooks the food inside. Even a 'simple' solar oven can reach temperatures of 275 degrees; that's hot enough to kill germs in water and certainly hot enough to cook food, though leaders might warn the children that the cooking process will take at least double the time that a regular oven at home would take. (Some things, like potatoes, might take even longer.)

General rule: Allow about one hour to preheat your oven, and cook food for at least twice as long as you would in a regular oven. (Be sure foods are thoroughly cooked before they are shared and eaten.)

What you need
- a cardboard box
- black construction paper or black paint and a brush
- aluminum foil
- stiff, clear plastic or heat-resistant glass
- non-toxic glue, tape, scissors
- a heat-resistant prop to hold up the box flap (the reflector)
- a sunny day

Optional
Insulate your oven by taping folded newspaper sheets around the box. This will help to retain the heat and cook your food more quickly.

Caution!

Observe strict safety rules as you supervise the use of a solar over. Do not allow young children to put food into the oven or to take food out. Assign the younger children other, equally important tasks, e.g. first taste!

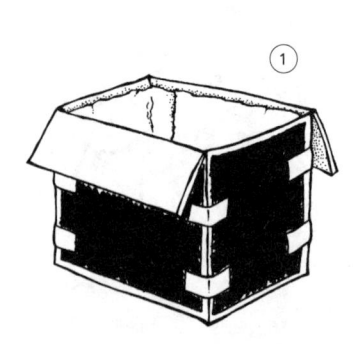

A New Day Enough

What you do
1. Paint the outside of your box black or tape black paper on the sides. (Black attracts the sunlight.) If you are painting the box, either leaders might do the painting ahead of time, or the children might paint the box in an earlier session (or Sunday school time). (1)
2. Line the inside of the box with aluminum foil.
3. On the top side of the box, mark a 2.5 cm border on all four sides. Cut along 3 sides, leaving the fourth side to create a flap.
4. Cover inside of flap with aluminum foil. (2)
5. Place water and/or foods in the oven.
6. Either cover the water/foods with the glass or stiff plastic, or for a more airtight condition, cover the open portion of the top of your oven with the plastic. (3)
7. Adjust the reflector and prop it so that it reflects the rays of the sun inside the box. (4)

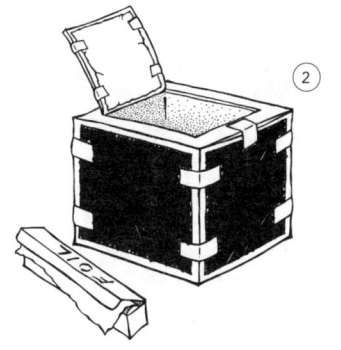

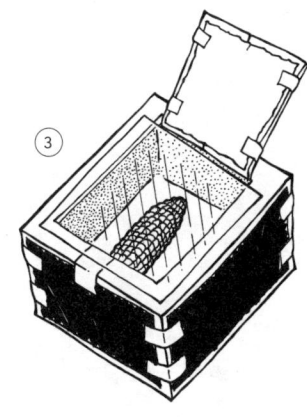

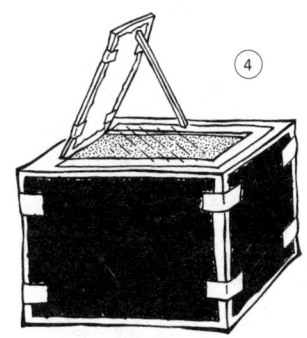

The sun's heat will cook hot dogs, chopped vegetables, corn on the cob, rice, potatoes–anything you like! You can make your oven more efficient by changing its shape, adding more insulation, making it more air tight, and using pots that are black on the outside. (Find out more at the library or check the Internet.)

Into the World: The Great Canadian Shoreline Cleanup

Every September, thousands of Canadians work together to clean up the shorelines in their communities. Joining citizens in 120 countries, 4½ million volunteers spend one week making shorelines of rivers, ponds, lakes, and oceans safer for fish, marine animals and birds, and people.

If you live near a shoreline, consider spending time with your group in cleaning up. If that is not possible, spend some time cleaning near your meeting place or learning more about where aquatic debris comes from and how it can be prevented. Invite individuals in your community who care about the environment to speak with the group.

Learn more by contacting the Vancouver Aquarium for information: online at: www.vanaqua.org/cleanup; or by mail: Great Canadian Shoreline Cleanup, Vancouver Aquarium Marine Science Centre, Box 3232, Vancouver, BC V6B 3X8. Phone: 1-877-427-2422.

A New Day
Enough

Water Tic Tac Toe
Goal: Check 5 squares in a row, down or across

- Ahead of time, leaders should research the facts behind the statements/concerns on the Water! gameboard (facing page).
- Photocopy the Water! gameboard (Make more than one copy if your group is large and invite the participants to form groups around each 'board.')
- Play this game with the participants and discuss the answers/concerns as you play.

Reproducible Activity Page — *A New Day* Enough

Water Tic Tac Toe

water

I can name the nearest river	I do not run the taps	I keep water in the fridge	I know what happens when I flush	I know the source of my drinking water
I pick up garbage when I hike	I have a favourite place near water	Free!	I know what H_2O means	I can name local fish species
I can name local water fowl	I know the temperature at which water boils	I can name the two great lakes in the NWT	I help keep the ice cube tray full	Free!
I do not put poisons down the drain or in the toilet	I never run a half full dishwasher	I love to swim, paddle, skate, row, and/or sail	I can name three oceans that touch Canada	I believe that water is precious
I don't call rainy weather "bad" weather	Free!	I don't waste water or ice	I can name all the oceans in the world	I try not to buy bottled water

19

The Egg • *A New Day*

The Egg

Once upon a time, under a shimmering full moon, a dove laid an amazing egg. It was not little and robin's-egg blue. It was not slippery with a black frog dot in the middle. And it was not white and ostrich-egg gigantic. No.

The nest was not amazing. The mother of this egg was not amazing. She looked plain, like every other dove in the world. The father wasn't particularly interesting to look at either.

But in the eyes of Love, who watches all the Earth with tenderness and compassion, all beings are beautiful. So, while the mother and father were ordinary, this really means that they were splendid and beautiful, because that is how Love works.

Justice, the father dove, and Hope, the mother, had been expecting an ordinary, brownish, oval egg. But this egg, laid in an ordinary nest in a tall maple tree, was not ordinary at all.

The eggshell was rainbow red and yellow, purple and green, blue and gold. On top of the radiant colours were marks. They were words: Sken:nen, Shalom, Salaam, Pax, Paz, Heiwa, and so on. Each word meant Peace as spelled in every language used by human creatures. (Other creatures do not need these scratchings, because the rainbow is enough. But Love, the Creator of all things, wanted to make sure that no one misunderstood the name of this egg.)

The sight of this Peace egg was so amazing that the wood ticks stopped ticking to take a look. Clouds laughed out loud. Crickets and grasshoppers went silent. On the end of a rich green maple leaf near the doves' nest, a grandmother spider looked at the egg and nodded. "At last," she whispered. "At last."

"What happened?" asked Justice. "I don't know," cooed Hope, "but I love this egg with all my heart. I'll care for it with all the tenderness inside me." Justice spread his wing over the egg and said, "Me, too."

Now the egg would have hatched in the beautiful maple tree, except that this tree was destined to be destroyed with the forest around it. The day after the egg was laid, logging machines shattered the stillness. Justice and Hope trembled with fear and with rage.

Grandmother spider called to the other spiders. "Come quickly!" she cried. The grandmother spiders came and began spinning and spinning. As the machines came closer, smashing down every tree in sight, the spiders spun faster, never

A New Day
The Egg

stopping. Grandfather spiders brought food and dew drops and gave neck massages to help. As the machines roared closer, spewing smoke and madness, the spiders quickly, but gently rolled the egg into the web-sack that was sturdy, strong, and soft. Not a second too soon, Justice grasped the end of the sack, and with Hope close by, left the ruined, weeping forest.

For days the doves searched for sanctuary. They wanted to find the perfect place, the safest and healthiest place to raise their baby. Everyone knows you must be brave to carry Peace. You must be brave to do things differently. And you must be brave to leave what is familiar and set out on a quest for new ways of being. Justice and Hope became tired, but they were brave and being brave made them strong.

Day after day they flew on. One afternoon, they found a factory in the country. "Could this be home?" Hope asked. But a ferocious armed guard yelled, "Off with you! We are busy making land mines and bombs so we can keep the world safe. Go away, stupid birds, or I'll shoot you!"

One morning, they found a house with a red geranium on the veranda far away from that factory. But there was fighting in that house, and the doves believed fighting is bad for babies. They flew on.

One evening they found a quiet park. "This looks good," sang Justice. But there were signs that even birds could read: poison on the grass, sewage in the water, and mosquito spray in the air. Wearily, Hope and Justice flew on.

It takes 14 days to hatch a dove egg. Justice and Hope knew that time was running out. Just when they thought their wings couldn't go up and down another minute, they saw a sign: City of Peace. "This will be it," Hope cooed. "Home at last."

Slowly they flew into the city. Gliding silently above the streets, they searched for a suitable tree or building. Suddenly, an explosion ripped through the air. It turned a street into rubble, knocked down a school, flattened a hospital. The explosion created a shock wave that spun Justice and Hope around in the air. Hope couldn't tell which way was up and which was down. Justice felt the web begin to slip. Spinning and falling, spinning and falling, Justice, Hope, and Peace unborn fell fast toward the stones and broken glass and rubble below. Most people were too busy to notice, but the children saw. With sinking hearts, they watched the doves, the web, and the egg hurtle through the dusty air.

The Peace egg landed, rolled, and stopped. Hope and Justice alighted beside it and checked quickly for cracks. The web was tattered.

First one shadow and then others fell over the doves and their precious egg. The shadows belonged to Compassion, Mercy, Humour, boys, and girls, "Look!" said a boy, "It's Peace!" Compassion asked, "Is he hurt?" A girl whispered, "Do you think she will stay?"

For a moment, all were silent. Hope looked at the rubble around her. Then she looked up at the children. "I think," she said, "that this is where we will raise our baby." Justice looked at her with fierce determination, and nodded. "But we'll need help," he said.

"We'll help you!" cried the children and the others. "Then Peace will grow here," said Justice. And Mercy, Compassion, Humour, and the children joined hands and danced to music they could hear above the fear right there in the brokenness and despair and rubble of the world.

A New Day
The Egg

Peacing It Together with Today

For many years newspapers and television reporters have told stories about violence in the Middle East. But what most of them have *not* told are stories about the thousands of peacemakers there! Every day, boys and girls, women and men are making peace. In daycares and schools, on the street and in communities, people are saying YES to peace.

At Givat Haviva, children come to a Jewish-Arab Centre for Peace. They write and make art to show that they want to live in a peaceful land. In Jerusalem (which means "City of Peace") young people bring their ideas of peace to an organization called Middle East Non-Violence and Democracy (MEND). They write radio plays and bring kids together by Internet to help keep people talking, even while violence is keeping them apart.

Neve Shalom/Wahat al-Salam is a small village half way between Tel Aviv and Jerusalem. Neve Shalom is Hebrew, and Wahat al-Salam is Arabic, and they mean the same thing in English–Oasis of Peace. Even though in other parts of Palestine and Israel there is violence between Arabs and Jews, at the Oasis of Peace people work, live, and play together. The school has two principals, one Jewish and the other Arab. In each classroom there are two teachers, one Jewish and one Arab. The children learn each other's languages, customs, cultures, and stories. They celebrate each other's holidays and festivals. They welcome visitors from all over the world who come to see this remarkable village of peace.

You can learn more about the Primary School and the School for Peace at Neve Shalom/Wahat al-Salam by visiting their website at www.nswas.org. You can also write to the children there to say hello. You might tell them what you are doing for peace in your community, or you might simply wish them Salam–Shalom–Peace! Their address is: Neve Shalom/Wahat al Salam, Doar Na Shimshon 99761, Israel.

In 2003, Raffi, the Canadian children's troubadour and peace advocate, recorded a song as a gift to the children of Israel and Palestine. It is called, "Salam, Shalom, Side by Side." You can download it for free from www.raffinews.com. (The children at the village listen to this CD, too.)

Crossword (see Reproducible Activity Page, page 27)

Photocopy this activity for each child, but encourage the children to help each other by working together, either in pairs or in small groups.

Solution

Peacing It Together with Our Faith

Steadfast love and faithfulness will meet; righteousness and peace will kiss each other.

(Psalm 85:10)

God promises and gives good things as people live in relationship with God and all of creation. Explain to the participants that the writer of this psalm believed that God was angry with people because they were not living in harmony with one another, with creation, and with God. The image of righteousness and giving the kiss of peace means that when people live as God calls us to live, we shall live in a land of peace. Invite the children to create a picture of a world living in harmony with God and at peace.

Crafting Peace: Raise a Flag for the World!

On page 26 in this book you will find the word "Peace" in many different languages. Invite the children to make a Peace banner or flag. Individual banners could be made or the children might work in pairs–as Justice and Hope worked together in the story–to create their messages of peace.

What you need
- a stick or dowel for each banner or flag
- fabric pens or pens with indelible ink in a variety of colours
- plain cotton cloth 30cm x 30cm or larger (This can be a piece of new fabric, or why not recycle an old shirt?)
- fabric glue

Note: If you are planning to dye the fabric first, plain cotton takes dye better than cotton blends. If you are tie dying, a peace image could be created during the dying process. (Check the Internet for tie dying ideas.)

What you do
- Colour an image of peace onto the fabric. (e.g. the doves from the story, a dove of your own design, the peace sign, a rainbow)
- Copy the different words for peace onto the flag.
- Mount your flag by tying it or gluing it to a stick or dowel.

Invite the children to display their flags in your meeting room, in the church sanctuary, at home, and in parades. They may want to make more than one flag to give away to people in the church, shut-in's, and to friends outside the church.

Into the World: Egg Gifts

You don't have to wait until Easter to make beautiful eggs! On page 61 you will find the names of dozens of people who are making peace in the world. Participants can also brainstorm together and come up with the name of one or more people in your community who are working to make peace–within families, with the environment, between people in communities, or on playgrounds and in schoolyards. Keeping these people in mind, make peace eggs, and give the eggs to them as a thank you for their work.

What you need
- 1 egg per participant
- food colouring
- bowls of water
- indelible marker
- a pin and a bowl
- small boxes/baskets to hold the decorated eggs
- fabric scraps to make "nests" for the eggs

What you do
- Use the pin to make a small hole in the top and bottom of each egg. Blow through one end until the yolk and white come out at the bottom. Catch this in the bowl!
- Wipe the egg clean.
- Add drops of dye to the bowls of water until the desired shades are achieved.
- Dip the egg into the dye baths, then allow the egg to dry. Using the indelible marker, write the name of a peacemaker on the egg and then all around the name, add the words for peace in as many languages as can fit on the egg. (See word list on page 26.)

When it has dried, place the egg in the "nest."

Meanwhile, with good supervision, invite participants to scramble the eggs. Turn on a stove to medium heat. Melt a little butter in a frying pan. Mix salt, pepper, and milk with the eggs and scramble with a fork. Put the egg mixture into the pan and stir until the eggs are cooked. Share and enjoy!

Wash the dishes and deliver the peace eggs to the peacemakers. Carefully!

Lafi Khotso Aman Pax Rongo Paci Heiwa Sulh Enh Keamanan Kimia Hoa binh

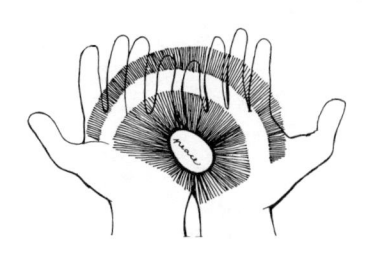

A New Day
The Egg

Saying "Peace" Around the World

Alafia [Yoruba (Nigeria)] • **Amahoro** [Rundi (Burundi)] • **Aman** [Urdu] • **Amani** [Swahili (Kenya, Tanzania)] • **Apirive** [Guarini (Paraguay)] • **Asomdwoe** [Twi-Akan (Ghana)] • **Baké** [Basque] • **Baris** [Turkish] • **Bekè** [Hungarian] • **Damai** [Malay/Indonesian] • **Eiphnh** [Greek] • **Emirembe** [Luganda (Uganda)] • **Enh taiwan** [Mongolian] • **Erkigsinek** [Inuit (Greenland)] • **Fandriampahalemana** [Malagasy (Madagascar)] • **Fifa** [Fon (Benin)] • **Filemu** [Samoan] • **Fred** [Norwegian/Danish] • **Friður** [Icelandic] • **Frieden** [German] • **Hacana** [Aymara (Bolivia)] • **Hau** [Tahitian] • **Heddwich** [Welsh] • **Heiwa** [Japanese] • **Here** [Bambara (Mali)] • **Hetep** [Egyptian] • **Hoa binh** [Vietnamese] • **Jam** [Fula (Guinea, Mali, Senegal)] • **Jamma** [Wolof (Senegal)] • **Katahimikan** [Tagalog (Philippines)] • **Keamanan** [Malay] • **Khotso** [Sesotho (Lesotho)] • **Khotso** [Tswana (Botswana)] • **Kimia** [Lingala (Zaire/Democratic Republic of Congo)] • **Kuthula** [Fanagolo (South Africa)] • **Lâfí** [Mossi (Ghana, Burkina Faso)] • **Lafiya** [Hausa (Nigeria)] • **Melino** [Tongan] • **Mier** [Slovak] • **Mir** [Czech] • **Mir** [Serb, Croat] • **Мир** [Russian (cyrillic alpha. For mir)] • **Nabada** [Somali] • **Nei** [Tangut (China)] • **Nyeinjaneyei** [Burmese] • **Pace** [Italian, Corsican, Romani] • **Paci** [Maltese] • **Paco** [Esperanto] • **Paix** [French] • **Pake** [Albanian] • **Pasch** [Romansch (Switzerland)] • **Pau he ping** [Mandarin] • **Pax** [Latin] • **Paz** [Portuguese] • **Paz** [Spanish] • **Phyongh'wa** [Korean] • **Pis** [Bislama (Vanuatu)] • **Pokój** [Polish] • **Qasikay** [Quecha (Mexico)] • **Rauha** [Finnish] • **Rongo** [Maori (NZ)] • **Runyararo** [Shona (Zimbabwe)] • **Salaam** [Arabi, Lebanese] • **Samadanam** [Tamil] • **Samaya** [Sinhalese] • **Santephiep** [Cambodian] • **Santiphap** [Thai, Lao] • **Selam** [Amharic (Ethiopia)] • **Shalom** [Hebrew] • **Shanti** [Hindi, Bengali] • **Sidi** [Tibetan] • **Sióchán** [Irish] • **Sken:nen** [Mohawk] • **Solh** [Dari] • **Sula** [Pushtu (Afghanistan)] • **Sulh** [Dari (Afghanistan)] • **Taika** [Lithuanian] • **Ukuthula** [Zulu] • **Vrede** [Afrikaans] • **Vrede** [Dutch] • **Yatanapa** [Pintupi (Australia)] • **Zaman** [Hausa (Nigeria)]

Crossword

Across

1. bird of peace
3. name of The Egg's mother (or the fourth candle of Advent)
5. don't stay
7. insects with 6 legs
10. Canadian tree
13. English word for Shalom
15. took wing
19. accept as true
21. what the Creator does; we do it too
22. female pronoun

Down

1. small speck
2. birds can lay one
4. fairness
6. spiders can spin this
8. talk to your Creator
9. male pronoun
11. it's on Canada's flag
12. single
14. young human
16. require
17. assist
18. opposite of "no"
20. an untruth

The Other Flood • *A New Day*

The Other Flood

Once upon a time, long, long ago, there was a wild and huge flood. Well, not soooo long ago. Not long ago like the Adam and Eve time, but not just last Tuesday, either. It was in between. This wasn't the Noah flood, and it wasn't the Nuh Flood story from the Koran, or the Manu and the Fish story from Hindu tradition. It wasn't the Aztec, Hopi, Haida or Babylonian Flood story, either. No.

This particular flood didn't get the kind of press those other stories did, but it happened just the same and it affected how things are.

This was a flood more or less like the one in the Bible, so everyone more or less knew how to play their parts: line up the saved people, line up the birds and insects and reptiles and animals, and check them off a list.

The unsaved ones knew the story, too. To make it an exciting story, their roles were to:

1. jeer at the ark
2. run around to the high hills, and
3. drown

All the saved ones lined up to get on the ark and walked, slithered, crawled, flew, waddled, and hopped up the ramp, right on cue. The ark filled quickly. The air resounded with honking, braying, roaring, squealing, barking, hissing, and meowing. It was a grand symphony!

There were others on the ark, too, quieter ones like Love and Peace, Goodness and Mercy, Sorrow and Joy, Wisdom and Justice. *Those* ones.

Just before the ramp went up, everyone lined up on the deck for roll call and shouted "Here!" at the appropriate time. Suddenly, Justice let out a fierce cry. "Wait!" he yelled. "We are missing Humour! We can't survive the trip without Humour!" And when Wisdom checked around, she found that Equality wasn't on board either.

Panic reigned. The rain rained. Everyone slipped and slid around, trying to hang over the railing, calling into the wet, purple dusk. For a long time they hissed, brayed, yelled, and roared: "Humour! Equality! Where are you?" But the only answer was the splash of rain on the slippery deck. They waited until the last possible moment, but the wind rose, and the night fell. The thunder spoke loud into the wide sky, and everyone knew they could wait no longer. The ramp was raised. The flood began. When that last bolt on the ramp found home, the history of the world changed.

For the usual 40 days and the usual 40 nights, the rain fell in torrents. People, animals, insects, reptiles, and birds dozed through most of it, waking every now again to grumble at their

A New Day
The Other Flood

neighbour, climb to a higher perch or crawl up to a higher bunk. Wisdom and Love found themselves in the bottom bunk, on the bottom floor, on the bottom of the ark. In the darkness, they waited.

Now, Equality and Humour knew that the ark had been built and that they were meant to be on it. The fact is they missed the boat because they were busy when the rain started. They were labouring to bring their baby Hope into the world.

Hope was born high above the floodwaters on the top of the highest mountain, in the highest mountain range in the world. (They don't even make mountains like that any more!) They were safe and dry in a cave on that mountain and could hardly wait for the 40 days to be up so they could find the others and be reunited with them. While they waited, they wrapped Hope in tenderness and invented songs for her. They created games and took turns making up stories and drawing pictures on the walls of the cave to amuse their beautiful little baby.

One day, the rain turned to fine mist, and the daylight seemed a little brighter. The ravens emerged from their berth and flew to the top of the ark. Hesitating only for a moment, they flew up and guided the ark between two hills. The rain stopped, the water went down, and the ark came to land. The ravens circled once in blessing and flew away. The sun broke through the clouds, and everyone filed off the ark into a lush, green valley.

Unlike other flood stories, these people didn't jump off the ark and plant gardens and crops. Nope. These individuals jumped off the ark, rolled up their sleeves, put on crabby faces, and grabbed hammers and shovels and wheelbarrows. Right away they built a wall.

After that, they built tiers so that some people could live above the others and could throw their leftovers and sewage on the ones below. And finally, they built laws so that half the people could not own property, vote, take part in religious ceremonies, or go to school. And because Equality and Humour were missing, the people didn't know any better. In fact, the people marched around thinking they were right, scowling and being dead serious about everything.

Whenever Justice or Love or Wisdom or Joy offered the people a different idea or a new way of doing things, they didn't smile at all. Instead, they crossed their arms, frowned, and scowled in disapproval right away. And that is how it was, you see. It was possible to catch a glimpse of Justice sometimes, but without Equality, it became problematic. It was possible to hear Wisdom's voice sometimes, but without Humour, no one wanted to listen very long.

For year after weary year that was the way of the world. It might have gone on that way forever except that during all this time, Equality and Humour had been travelling down the mountain toward the village gate, carrying Hope. When they finally reached the valley, they knocked on the gate. They were happy and excited to tell everyone that they had survived the flood and that they had Hope.

When the village people answered the gate, they stood with their arms folded across their chests and scowled and frowned. The first one said, "People here don't need Humour or Equality or Hope. The stock market is doing very well

30

without you!" The second one said, "We're making progress here. Don't waste our precious time!" The third one said, "You are the wrong colour, the wrong age, the wrong faith, the wrong language group, the wrong gender, and there is nothing that you have that we want. Go away!"

Then they slammed that gate, straightened their shoulders, and went back to supervising the construction of a new wall. They were so busy and so crabby that they did not know that their actions had five witnesses: one girl, one boy, Justice, Love, and Wisdom.

Now, five is not a big, powerful group. For example, five cannot knock down a tiny wall, let alone a big one. And these five knew it was almost impossible to change things with logical arguments. (They'd tried, but it's hard to change without Equality, Humour, and Hope.)

But these five decided to spread the word about what they had seen. They told one villager that Equality, Humour, and Hope were out in the world, alive. And then they said, "Pass it on!"

And over time, from the first flood stories until at least last Tuesday, that word has spread in a painting, quilt pattern, sidewalk chalk drawing, story, song or hug. Equality, Humour, and Hope are still at the gate, waiting to be welcomed in. We need them. Pass it on!

A New Day
The Other Flood

Peacing It Together with Today

One hundred years ago, a Canadian heroine changed the world with humour and hard work. Her name was Nellie.

Nellie McClung grew up in a time when women weren't even allowed to vote! She decided to change that. With her faith and her friends, Nellie helped Manitoba become the first province or territory in Canada where women could elect politicians. That was in 1916! Later, Nellie and the group known as The Famous Five succeeded in changing Canadian laws so that women were able to take part at all levels of government. Nellie used all of her talents as a journalist, speaker, suffragette, novelist, and reformer. (One reform she worked for was free medical and dental care for children.) She spent her life working to create a better world for the generations to follow.

Most famously, Nellie used humour in a play titled **"The Woman's Parliament"** to educate others about the injustice of not allowing women to vote. In 1914, in a packed theatre, Nellie and her friends took the roles of female parliamentary leaders debating whether to allow *men* to vote. Their play was hilarious and well received. The following year, the government was voted out of office, and in 1916 the new government gave the vote to Manitoba women!

Nellie learned about speaking up for what she believed was right. When she was just starting out she said, "For the first time I saw the power of speech. I saw faces brighten, eyes glisten, and felt the atmosphere crackle with new power. I saw what could be done with words, for I had a vision of a new world as I talked."

Craig Kielburger knows about the power of words, too. He has been changing the world since he was 12-years-old. One morning Craig reached for the comics section of the newspaper and saw a headline, "Battled Child Labour, Boy 12, Murdered!" Craig was curious to know more. What is child labour? Why would a boy 12-years-old get murdered because of it? When Craig researched the questions, he learned that there are more than 250 million child labourers in the world, many working in horrible conditions. With his friends he began a group called Kids Can Free the Children. In six years, the organization spread to 35 countries and today involves more than 100,000 children and youth.

Both Nellie and Craig learned that it is possible to change the world. It takes organization, belief that the work can be done, help from friends, and a willingness to speak up.

Speaking up is scary for a lot of us. We get butterflies or feel as if we've got the dreaded *jelly belly!* But everyone feels this way at first, and even seasoned speakers sometimes feel nervous. That's normal. Here are a few tips to help speakers gain more confidence:

1. Do your research so that you know what you're talking about.
2. Keep a sense of humour and perspective–everyone makes mistakes.
3. Practise your speech over and over again.
4. Think about joining a debating club or public speaking club to get lots of practice.

Public Speaking

Why is it when I stand to speak
My voice comes out a whisper?
Hands are shaking
Knees are quaking
I wish that I were crisper!

Write a poem that tells how you feel when you have to speak in public.

Word Find (see page 36 and the Reproducible Activity Page, page 37)
Invite the children to complete the Word Find.

> Note: There is an excellent book for kids who want to change the world. It's called *Take Action! A Guide to Active Citizenship* by Marc and Craig Kielburger (Toronto: Gage Learning 2002). It includes all sorts of tips to help you hold meetings, make speeches, write letters, conduct surveys, and raise public awareness and support. (A follow-up resource, *Take More Action*, is an advanced guide to global citizenship.)

Peacing It Together with Our Faith

> *These are the things that you shall do: Speak the truth to one another, render in your gates judgments that are true and make for peace.*
>
> (Zechariah 8:16)

God calls us to speak the truth and work for peace.

Play a game that allows the children to speak the truth and have some fun: Select a "truth object" to hide and designate a "peace base" where all the children can gather. Choose one player to hide the truth object while the others close their eyes or leave the room–no peeking! Everyone looks for the hidden truth object and when anyone finds it, they run to the peace base shouting, "Equality, Humour, and Hope!" It is then the finder's turn to hide the object. Play may continue as long as the children are having fun.

Crafting Peace: Make Paper and Save a Tree!

One of the causes of flooding is soil erosion. One of the causes of erosion is deforestation. One of the causes of deforestation is logging for pulp and paper.

By using recycled paper, we can make an important contribution to keeping forests alive. You can create your own paper from waste paper. You can make your paper interesting and beautiful (e.g. by adding leaves and flower petals).

What you need
- scrap paper (newspaper, tissue paper, anything that isn't waxy)
- bucket with warm water
- an iron
- a sponge
- two wooden frames of the same size (e.g. old picture frames)
- fibreglass window screening slightly larger than your frames
- staples or tacks (for attaching screening to one frame)
- a plastic tub or basin, large enough to hold the frames
- about 10 pieces of flannelette cloth or white felt slightly larger than your frames
- 2 cookie sheets or boards slightly larger than your frames

Optional
- kitchen blender (this speeds up the process)
- liquid starch (such as the water you save after boiling potatoes for dinner) (starch helps create a smoother surface on the paper)

What you do
1. Tear the scrap paper into tiny pieces and soak the pieces in the bucket of warm water.
2. Tack or staple the screen to one frame. Make it as tight as possible. (1)
3. Make the pulp. There are two ways. The fast way is to put wet, ripped paper and warm water into a blender (to half full). Run the blender slowly, then increase the speed until the pulp is smooth. (You will need to do this about three times to make sufficient pulp.) The slower way is to soak the torn paper overnight. Then take handfuls of the soaked paper and rub or pound it to a pulp on cement or a rough stone.
4. Half fill the basin with warm water. Add several cups of pulp and stir.
5. Add about 2 tablespoons of starch.

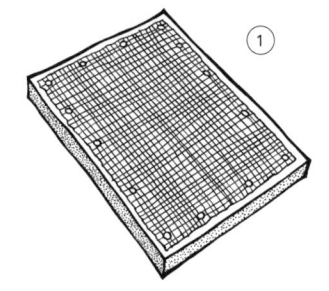

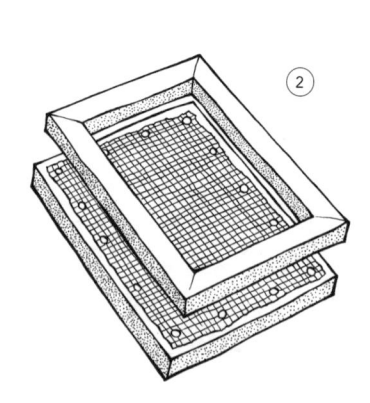

6. Spread newspapers on the floor and place one cookie sheet on them. (Making paper is messy!)
7. Place the empty frame on top of the screened frame (2) and lower both, held together, into the pulp. Level out the pulp while the frames are submerged by gently rocking the frames back and forth until the pulp looks even. Raise the frames gently and allow the water to drip, drip, drip through the screen. (3)
8. Remove the empty top frame.
9. Gently place the edge of the screened frame, now carrying a layer of paper, onto one piece of cloth, then ease the frame down flat, with the paper directly on the fabric. Use the sponge to press out as much water as possible. (Squeeze the water back into the basin.)
10. Slowly lift the edge of the frame, leaving the sheet of wet paper on the fabric. Move the fabric and paper to the cookie sheet.
11. Repeat steps 7 to 10, stacking the wet sheets between fabric pieces until you have about 10 sheets of paper. Place a board or second cookie sheet on top of the pile and press out the excess water by standing on it.
12. Gently peel apart your wet sheets of paper. Spread them out to dry. Iron them if you like.

Congratulations! You've used your creativity and helped save a tree!

Into the World: Working for Equality

Nellie McClung believed that Equality was just outside the gates of the village and so she opened the gate and invited Equality to live in Canada. Women got the vote! One hundred years later, Craig Kielburger believed that Freedom is just outside the gates of the village and he has opened the gate and invited in Freedom for children.

Who do you believe is just outside the gate? Who would you like to invite into our lives?

Using paint, pencil crayons or other art supplies, play with your ideas. You might want to create artwork for your meeting place. Or, you might like to create art to send to someone you think is making the world safer for children. You might like to create a one-of-a-kind postcard for Craig Kielburger at Free the Children. The address is: Kids Can Free the Children, 50 High Oak Trail, Richmond Hill, ON L4E 3L9.

A New Day
The Other Flood

Solution

```
G O D X F L O O D E D Y
I N A M I N U T E Q U E
R A I N S H U M O U R S
L A M P S O Z E B A R C
E M M A C P A T S L U R
S P E A C E S T M I R I
F E R D C B S H U T A E
G H C A V E I J K Y E S
B O Y R O Q P G O N M L
E V U T T S L A U G H S
S W X Y E Z A T B C X A
T E L L G E D E V E R Y
```

Word Find (see Reproducible Activity Page, facing)

Photocopy the Word Find (facing page). Children might like to have individual Word Find pages to work with, or they might enjoy working in pairs or small groups. Be open to their preference, but encourage sharing and working together. Point out how finding solutions is easier when people work as a team.

Word Find

Find the words:

GO	PEACE	TELL
GOD	MERCY	VOTE
FLOOD	ME	LAUGHS
GIRL	CRIES	GATE
RAIN	SHUT	EVERY
EQUALITY	CAVE	SAY
HUMOUR	BOY	YES
HOPE	BEST	

G	O	D	X	F	L	O	O	D	E	D	Y
I	N	A	M	I	N	U	T	E	Q	U	E
R	A	I	N	S	H	U	M	O	U	R	S
L	A	M	P	S	O	Z	E	B	A	R	C
E	M	M	A	C	P	A	T	S	L	U	R
S	P	E	A	C	E	S	T	M	I	R	I
F	E	R	D	C	B	S	H	U	T	A	E
G	H	C	A	V	E	I	J	K	Y	E	S
B	O	Y	R	O	Q	P	G	O	N	M	L
E	V	U	T	T	S	L	A	U	G	H	S
S	W	X	Y	E	Z	A	T	B	C	X	A
T	E	L	L	G	E	D	E	V	E	R	Y

Dragons • *A New Day*

Dragons

In the olden days, when people still believed in war and thought it was all right to pollute the world if you were rich, there lived a boy and a girl who were best friends. They changed the world.

The boy's name has long been forgotten and the girl's name, too. This happens sometimes. So, in this story, we must simply call them Boy Child and Girl Child. You might want to give the boy or girl your own name for this story.

The village where the children lived was surrounded by neat fields of sunflowers and wheat on three sides. On the fourth side there was a beautiful forest. At the forest edge lived an old woman whose name we do remember, Martha. She was a gardener who gave fresh herbs and healing plants to anyone who asked. The children stopped by her house often because she was kind and told them stories.

Deep in that forest there was a fresh green pond where silver and golden fishes lived. Around it, juicy red raspberries grew in abundance. Birds of every colour of the rainbow raised their babies in the trees. The sharp-eared fox, clever raccoon, majestic bear, and singing cricket lived there with all the other creatures. The children went there often because the forest was kind and let them swim and watch animals.

One day, it was a Tuesday, just when the steeple bells struck 11 o'clock, the earth shook, and the air grew hot. A great, fire-breathing, red-winged, white-clawed, scaly-skinned, humungous dragon arrived on the road to the village. The village people left their fields, ran like the wind into their houses, and slammed their doors tight.

That dragon walked past the neat fields, nifty barns, and tidy houses and went into the forest. And that is where he stayed.

The village people peeped out of their windows and then tiptoed into the village square. The blacksmith said that he'd just completed a shiny new sword. "I think it could slay a dragon. Let's try it out!" A farmer said he'd rather get drunk so he didn't have to think about dragons. A shopkeeper thought people should pray to God to save them. A few put their belongings on a wagon and went away. Most people returned to their fields and pretended that they had never seen a dragon at all.

But the mayor and the blacksmith were wondering about that sword. "Let's get George from the next village to come and kill the dragon. We could pay him and give him medals or something," said the

A New Day
Dragons

blacksmith. The mayor thought this was a grand idea. He sent a runner racing to get George. The blacksmith gave him the sword and told him to kill the dragon.

George ran into the forest and waged a mighty battle. And even though part of the forest got burned, the banks of the pond caved in, and many animals died, George killed the dragon and cut off his head.

The village people were so delighted that they gave cherry pies to the blacksmith and to George. They named George a saint. Then they went back to their farms, happy.

The next Tuesday, about 11 o'clock, a new dragon stomped through the village, just like the other one, and moved into the forest. The village people knew just what to do. Some pretended they hadn't seen it, some got drunk so they wouldn't have to think about dragons, some prayed, some hid, some ran, the blacksmith made a sword, and the runner went to find George. Then, George ran into the forest and waged a mighty battle. Even though part of the forest got burned, the banks of the pond caved in, and many of the animals died, George killed the dragon and cut off his head.

The village people were so delighted that they named their church, "St. George the Dragon-Slayer Church." They baked raspberry pies for him and the blacksmith, and went back to their farms, happy.

The next Tuesday, about 11 o'clock, another dragon stomped through the village, just like the others, and moved into the forest. The village people knew exactly what to do. They were very good at it, even. Some pretended, some got drunk, some prayed, some hid, some ran, the blacksmith made a sword, and the runner went to find George. George went into the forest and waged a mighty battle. Even though part of the forest got burned, the banks of the pond caved in, and many of the animals died, George killed the dragon and cut off his head.

Once again, the job was done, the village was safe, and the people were happy. This time, they decided to commission some lovely stained glass windows for their church. These windows would show George with a dragon's head and a sword; people would come from all over to see them.

A few days later, while the village people were examining the window designs, Boy Child said to Girl Child, "I don't think this system is working very well." Girl Child nodded. "Every time George kills the dragon, another one comes." And so they asked to speak to the people. The mayor was surprised, but he agreed.

"We don't think this dragon-slaying business is working very well," said Girl Child.

The blacksmith said, "You are only children. If you want to talk, say something nice."

"But if you keep killing dragons, another one just takes its place," said Boy Child.

"Whose children are these? Put them to bed or something," yelled a man.

"We want to try something different if another dragon comes," Boy Child said. "We have a new idea," Girl Child added.

The village people began to mumble and grumble. They didn't like new ideas. And anyway, they had a system that worked:

1. blacksmith makes sword
2. mayor sends for George

3. George slays dragon with sword
4. village people pay George and blacksmith

Suddenly, the clock struck 11.00. The mayor jumped six inches into the air. "Oh, oh!" he said. "What day is this?" Then the earth shook, and the air grew hot. "Enough talk! Get George!" hollered the mayor. "Please!" said Boy Child. "Can't we get Martha this time?"

"Pish posh!" said the blacksmith. "Martha is a gardener. She knows nothing at all about dragon-slaying." The other villagers followed their routine: they ran, drank, hid, pretended. The blacksmith ran for a sword. The mayor ran to make up an order for pies. The runner went to find George.

When George arrived he was surprised to be met by Boy Child and Girl Child. "We have a better plan," they said. "It includes Martha–because two heads are better than one, right?"

George didn't look convinced, but before the blacksmith could arrive with the sword, Boy Child and Girl Child took George's hand, and they all ran as fast as they could to Martha's house. "Please," they cried. "There's another dragon in the forest. Can you go with George this time?"

"You believe I can help?" Martha asked. "Yes," they said, even though they were actually not one hundred per cent sure, only ninety-nine per cent.

Martha and George (minus his sword) went into the forest to meet the dragon. The children went back to wait in the village square. Soon the village people joined them to find out what had happened. "Martha is in the forest with the dragon!" shouted a woman. "Then I guess we should plan her funeral," said a man rolling his eyes. "We'll bury her at St. George the Dragon-Slayer Church," mused the mayor. "That would be fitting." The village people sat and planned what they would sing and who would dig the grave. "She always was a bit off," said a man. "That's right. It's not our fault," said the mayor. "We had a very good system for dragons."

Meanwhile, the blacksmith with the sword was still looking for George.

The clock struck noon. And then 1:00. Then 2:00. Then 3:00.

"I don't hear any fighting or chewing," said a man. The clock struck 4:00. Then 5:00. The village people were planning the fine details of Martha's funeral. They were at the part about what kind of flowers they might put around her grave when Boy Child announced, "Here they come!"

The village people rushed to the edge of the square and peered into the gathering night. Martha was leading that great dragon out of the forest, slowly. "What happened?" cried the blacksmith. "She tamed him!" smiled George.

What took place next is hard to believe, but it happened just the same. First the children and then the others learned to live with the dragon, and the dragon learned to live with the people. The blacksmith took home the unused sword and began making garden hoes.

A New Day
Dragons

Next, they all became friends. The dragon decided to help the village people by keeping their homes warm with his hot breath. He lit their stoves every morning so they could make nice oatmeal porridge for breakfast. In return, the village people told stories to the dragon and fed him delicious soups and chocolate cake, because that's what dragons like best.

The village became the envy of all the other villages around. Everyone wanted to have a dragon, now that people knew how to behave with one.

Today, if you travel to Tarascon in the south of France, you can visit St. Martha's Church. In that church is a stained glass window showing Martha and the dragon. In many countries, you can see churches named after St. George, too. No church that I know about has been named for Boy Child and Girl Child. Yet.

Maybe some day, we will name a peace park for Boy Child and Girl Child because in the olden days, when people still believed in war and thought it was all right to pollute the world if you were rich, they changed the world. When they grew up, Boy Child and Girl Child had many children. Some say that if you look quickly in a mirror, you can catch a glimpse of one of them out of the corner of your eye.

Peacing It Together with Today

To reach the town of Cochrane, Alberta from Calgary, you head west toward the Rocky Mountains. At the top of a hill you see Cochrane laid out beneath you. Beyond it are the majestic, snow-capped mountains. Ranching country spreads north, south, and west through the foothills. The Bow River winds through the town, bringing fresh water from the mountains. Ordinary Canadians live, work, go to school, and play here. But one thing makes Cochrane different—and it's attracting a lot of attention. It's what people there are doing about bullies.

One day, Bill Belsey, an educator and father, asked himself three questions: "What has God given me that I can use to give back to the community? How could I help create a safe, positive, environment in Cochrane? How could I inspire others to help?" He decided to speak to the mayor and councillors. He asked, "Is bullying an issue we need to address as a community?" They answered, "Yes!"

Soon, an anti-bullying task group formed. Twenty students (from elementary and high schools) formed The Youth Action Committee. They are tackling the problem by writing and performing skits and plays, then talking about the issue. They have created a Public Service Announcement (PSA) about bullying that runs in the local theatre. Their website www.bullying.org received one million visits from throughout Canada and around the world *in one month!*

In 2002, Mayor Judy Stewart made a declaration: "I call upon citizens to recognize bullying for the societal problem that it is. I call upon you to make a difference by taking the time to get involved. I call upon you to encourage all Canadians to help make our country bully free."

In 2003, November 16 to November 22 was declared "Bullying Awareness and Prevention Week." This raised awareness about the serious impact that bullying behaviours have on society and encouraged people to explore and share solutions about how bullying can be prevented.

Copy and use the Anti-Bullying Pledge from the Cochrane website (or see page 44), or consider creating a group version of your own.

Anti-Bullying Pledge

This is for me,
my friends today,
and my friends tomorrow.

I think being mean stinks!

I won't watch someone get picked on
Because **I am a do-something perso**n,
not a do-nothing person.

I care
I *can* help change things
I can be a leader

In my world there are <u>no bullies allowed</u>.

Bullying is bad
Bullying bites
Bullying bothers me.

**I know sticking up for
someone is the right thing
to do**.

My name is _____
and I **won't** stand by

I will stand up.

When you drive from Calgary to Cochrane, you will see something new. Attached to the gigantic "Welcome" sign, you will see another sign. It reads, "Cochrane: A Community Striving to be Bully Free."

A New Day
Dragons

Word Play

Write out the words PEACEMAKER and TRANSFORMATION on a flip chart. Invite some discussion about what the words mean. Ask the children to copy the words on paper then work out how many different words can be made from PEACEMAKER and TRANSFORMATION. Encourage children to work together. (It is also fun to use Scrabble Tiles for this activity.)

Copy this page so that children can compare their word findings.

PEACEMAKER

5 letters
cream
creek
maker
peace

4 letters
cake
came
keep
mace
make
meek
pear
peek
peer
rake
ream
reek

3 letters
ace
ape
arm
cap
car
ear
eek
map
mar
Pam
pea
per
ram

2 letters
am
me

TRANSFORMATION

9 letters
formation
transform

6 letters
format
nation

5 letters
trams
first
moist
moons
moors
Norma
rafts
rants
rifts
rooms
start
storm
tarts

4 letters
raft
firs
form
fort
moon
moor
moot
morn
most
mast
noon
rams
rant
rats
rift
rims
room
root
sift
soft
star
tart
torn
tram

3 letters
fan
far
fir
fat
for
nor
ram
ran
rat
rim
tin
mat
man
aft
ant

2 letters
on
am
an
it

Note: There are words other than listed here that can be made from PEACEMAKER and TRANSFORMATION. Older children might be given this challenge—with or without the use of a dictionary.

45

A New Day
Dragons

Dragon Drama
The story *Dragons* will work well as a drama. It may be rewritten with lines for each actor or narrated while the actors mime the action. The group might like to practise and perform it for the young people in the neighbourhood, for their church congregation(s), or for parents at a party. (Since there is no limit to the number of Villagers required, as many children as would like a part may take part.)

Characters
Dragon (one dragon may play the part of all the dragons; there is never more than one on stage at a time)
Martha
George
Mayor
Blacksmith
Runner
Villagers (3 or more)
Boy Child
Girl Child

Props
- a sword for George
- a chain of office for the mayor
- a basket of vegetables/plants for Martha
- hats for the village people

Adding sound effects enhances the production–just use your imagination!

In one production in Calgary, Andrew was the Dragon. He made his own dragon head by attaching long white felt fangs to the peak of a green baseball hat. He cut out two big circles from white fabric and glued black dots on them to make the eyes; these were glued to the upper part of the cap. During each "fight," the dragon and George went behind a screen, so the audience could not see them. Every time George "cut off the dragon's head," Andrew tossed his hat in the air above the screen!

Peacing It Together with Our Faith

Blessed are the peacemakers, for they will be called children of God.
(Matthew 5:9)

This verse is one of The Beatitudes, part of Jesus' Sermon on the Mount. Being "blessed" does not mean that God will give something to peacemakers. Here "blessed" means "happy." Those who are peacemakers are happy and are in a close relationship with God.

Invite participants to create a blessing for God. What could they say, write, sing, dance, or do that would make God happy?

Crafting Peace: War Toys into Art

In Brantford, Ontario, there is a statue of Mohawk leader Joseph Brant. It is made out of cannons that were melted down and recast into a statue. In Oakland, California, the Fruitvale Elementary School exchanged their toy weapons, violent DVDs, and video games for books and pencils. In Cambodia, art student Kim Samdy took an AK-47 assault rifle and created a beautiful bird sculpture. In Courtenay, British Columbia, artist MacKenzie Duncan used an army shirt to create an interesting pink-lined skirt.

"…they shall beat their swords into ploughshares…." (Isaiah 2:4)

The prophet Isaiah had a dream that one day people would end war. He imagined that we would take all the swords of war, melt them down, and make them into ploughshares to plough the fields and plant crops like wheat to grow food. Turning something violent into something peaceful is a powerful idea. Invite the participants to turn their "swords" into "ploughshares."

Ask them to "turn in their weapons" and create a peace sculpture out of war toys and violent videos and DVDs. Brainstorm how this might be done as a group project. Decide on a symbol of peace that could be created using glue, wire, hammers, and nails. The children might make flowerpots or garden boxes. A display at a school, where your faith community meets, or other places could be arranged.

Into the World: Questioning Violence in Media

We are careful to put good, healthy food into our bodies. We are careful to drink water that is clean and pure. But when it comes to what we put into our minds and hearts, sometimes we forget to be careful. Sometimes we feed our minds junk!

A lot of junk food for the mind and heart comes from violent DVDs, video games, and television programs. People who make violent games and toys for kids get rich–while the world gets more violent and kids' minds get filled up with violence, sexism, racism, and greed–all toxic junk!

Ask the participants if they have ever noticed how small children copy what they see on television (clothes, behaviour, language). What defences do we have against mind junk? We can become critical thinkers and help young people become critical, too.

Invite children to create a list of 10 popular shows and respond to the following questions for each one. Send copies of your survey to your local television station, your local newspaper, or your school newspaper.

1. Name of television show
2. Total number of ads during the program
3. What products were the ads trying to get us to buy?
4. Does this program have a product? (For example, are the producers trying to get you to buy a doll or toy that is specifically related to the show?)
5. How is conflict solved on the program?
6. What does the story teach?
7. If there is environmental damage in the story, how do the characters respond to it?
8. How are women and girls portrayed in the story? Do they think and act independently or are they decorations and victims?
9. How many instances of violence are shown on the program?
10. How are different races portrayed? What colour is the "good guy"? What colour is the "bad guy"?

Discuss the results among participants. Rate the program on a scale of 1 to 10, with 10 being a program that reflects one's values most highly.

A New Day
Dragons

Take the Ten-Day TV-Free Challenge!

In one Quebec school the kids led the parents, churches, and local businesses in becoming involved in the challenge. Students used their free time for dance lessons, indoor hockey, picnics, campfires, music, and sing-alongs. The whole community celebrated!

Ask the children to consider: Could you do it? Could you and your classmates organize a ten-day challenge? What would you miss most? What could you do with the extra time that you are currently using by sitting in front of the television?

The Wall • *A New Day*

The Wall

Once upon a time when grandmothers knew how to knit and grandfathers knew how to whittle, there was a little old man and a little old woman who always carried a bag. In it were marvellous things for boys and girls. They carried that bag everywhere they went, and whenever it seemed right, they would give something from the bag to a child.

One day the little old man went to the mailbox and discovered a curious letter. He carried it into the kitchen where the little old woman was pouring two cups of hot tea. He read the letter out loud.

"Dear friends," he read. "We have heard that you carry a special bag. Could you take your bag to the children on the other side of the mountain? It would be best if you could hurry." And that was all. There was no signature or return address. The little old man and the little old woman sipped their tea in silence and thought for a while. And then they put on their jackets, picked up the bag, and walked out the door.

The bag wasn't all that big, just big enough. It didn't look special. But inside the bag were the most special things the little old people could find in the whole wide world. There were songs about love and laughter, sadness and hope. There were songs to help you snuggle down on a nice soft lap and feel cozy. Inside those songs you could get lost for a while and find your heart.

There were stories in the bag, too. Stories about clear lakes, deep forests, and children growing up free. Stories about jumping over the moon, working inside a mountain, and living under the sea. Some stories were short, like a hop. Others were as long as a country road. Inside the stories you could get lost for a while and find your imagination.

And that's not all. The little old man and the little old woman had tucked dreams inside the bag, too. These were dreams about changing from one thing to another, finding what was lost or starting things never heard of before. Some dreams went on the whole night-long; others were so tiny that several could fit into an afternoon nap.

The little old man and the little old woman had been giving their gifts to children for a long time, but they had never been over the mountain and they were excited to go there. For days and days they walked toward that mountain. But one Tuesday morning, about 11 o'clock, they found they could go no farther. They had come upon a great, big wall.

The wall was taller than the sun, deeper than the ocean, and wider than an owl's eyes could see.

A New Day
The Wall

The little old man and the little old woman stopped and put down their stories and songs and dreams. "What will the children do if we can't get over the mountain?" asked the little old woman. "We must think fast," said the little old man, "The letter said that we should hurry."

After they had been thinking for about 43 minutes, the little old man saw a car coming lickety-split down the road. When it stopped, a man got out. "Look!" said the little old man. "It's an expert!"

He could tell that the man was an expert because the man wore important clothes and had a cell phone stuck in his ear.

"Please help," said the little old woman. "We need to get past this wall so we can visit the children on the other side of the mountain."

The expert glanced at the old people, then his cell phone rang. He had a long, loud, expert conversation. After he finished, he agreed with the little old man and the little old woman that they did indeed have a problem.

"I'll check my day-timer. We could do lunch, maybe next week or next year. E-mail your cell number, and I'll have my people call yours," he said. And he climbed expertly back into his shiny car and drove away.

The old people sat down to think. Suddenly the little old woman stood up and pointed. "Look!" she said, "Here come some rich people. Surely they will help us."

The rich people stopped their long, shiny car and pressed buttons to open the windows. "Please," said the little old woman, "could you help?"

The rich woman stared at the dusty old people. Their clothes were plain and poor. "Squeegee kids are mighty old these days," she said. The rich man held out a handful of nickels. "Here you are," he said. "Just don't scratch the windshield."

"Money won't help us," said the little old man. "What we need is to get past this wall. It's the children...."

A phone rang in the car. "It's your broker, darling," said the rich woman. The rich man began to roll up his window. "Goodbye," he said. "Good luck with your little project!" He put the phone to his ear, his foot on the gas pedal, and was gone.

The little old people sat on the grass. The little old woman patted the little old man's wrinkled hand. "Something will come along soon," she said, trying to sound hopeful.

And something did. A big army tank rumbled slowly toward them, breaking the pavement as it came. Its deafening roar shook butterflies and birds right out of the trees.

The big army tank stopped by the old people. The top popped open. "Want anyone killed?" asked the general. "No!" cried the little old man. "We want to get past this wall so we can visit the children on the other side of the mountain."

"Hmm," said the general. "Well, I could blast a hole through it. I could knock it down, bomb it, smash it to smithereens for you. Actually," he said smiling. "It might be fun!"

52

A New Day
The Wall

"No, no!" cried the little old man. "Please don't do that! There might be children on the other side!"

"And lakes and snakes, and trees and bees and frogs and dogs!" added the little old woman. The general looked puzzled. "Well," he said, "if you don't want me to kill anybody, and you don't want me to bomb the wall, I guess I'll be going." He ducked down, the lid clanged shut, and the tank rumbled slowly away.

The little old man sank slowly onto the grass again. "I guess there's only us," he said sadly. "But I don't think we're much use against this mighty, big wall."

"I know," sighed the little old woman, "but sitting here isn't good for the arthritis." She pulled him to his feet, and they walked to the wall, looked it up and down and sighed. And then they noticed something.

The wall looked like one smooth surface, but in the evening sunlight, when they looked very carefully, they discovered that the wall was made of tiny bits. Tiny bits like pebbles.

"And look!" cried the little old woman. "If you hold your head just so, you can see something. You can see writing on this wall." "Aha!" cried the little old man, and he read the words out loud: "Fear. Pollution. Racism. Sexism. Stubbornness. Ignorance. Greed."

"Imagine that!" the little old woman exclaimed. "Why, it's not one big thing after all. It's just a lot of little bitty things. Come on, old man, let's see what we can do!" And she winked at the little old man, and he winked back at her. Together, they worked and worked until they pulled out a tiny bit of Fear. Next, they pulled out a tiny bit of Greed.

Soon, the bright moon rose in the sky. By her light the old people counted. They'd only managed to pull out five bits. "Oh dear," said the little old woman, "I don't think we'll live long enough to make a hole in this wall. We're already very old."

The little old man tenderly rubbed her shoulders. "There, there," he said. "We're just tired. Let's each take a dream out of our bag. That will make us feel better." And they curled up together under the moon and went to sleep.

The little old man dreamed about boys and men who could break down walls. He dreamed about Martin Luther King Jr., Nelson Mandela, and Gandhi. He dreamed about Jim Endicott, Lester B. Pearson, Kevin Thomas, and Dan Berrigan. He saw visions of David Swann, Craig Kielburger, David Suzuki, Georges Erasmus, and Dow Marmur.

The little old woman dreamed about girls and women who could break down walls. She dreamed about Mairead Corrigan, Rachel Carson, and Karen Hamdon. She dreamed about Lorraine Sinclair, Sally Armstrong, Ursula Franklin, and Nellie McClung. She saw visions of Pauline Johnson, Barbara Shoomski, Lois Wilson, Jane Goodall, and Rosa Parks.

In the morning, the little old man and the little old woman told stories about all the people they had dreamed of.

At breakfast, she told about Dr. Helen Caldicott from Australia. She works to save children from nuclear poisons.

At lunch, he told about Raffi and Bruce Cockburn from Canada. They sing love songs for the Earth.

At dinner, they talked about Diane and Andreas

A New Day
The Wall

D'Souza in India. They make safe spaces for people to work for world peace.

After that, the little old people felt about 100 years younger, so they went straight back to work pulling out bits of Greed and Pollution from that gigantic wall. In fact, the dreams made them feel so good that they sang a little old song right there by that ugly big wall. And that's when things changed.

People began coming by to find out what was going on. "Why are you singing by the wall?" asked a man with a blue hat. "Don't you know that the situation is ugly, terrible, and hopeless?"

A big girl said, "It's useless to even try!" A big boy rolled his eyes. "Bleak," he said. "Waste of time."

A woman with a red hat looked at the old people and shook her head sadly. "They've gone crackers," she said. "Picking away at a wall like that is a waste of time. They should be put safely away where there are lots of rocking chairs."

In the sudden silence that fell, all the people heard a little sound, a tiny sound, like this: *chip, chip, chip*. "What's that?" asked a little young boy, pressing his ear to the wall. "I heard it, too," said a little young girl. The teeny tiny sound was coming from the other side of the wall. The little young girl and the little young boy began to chip, chip, chip at the wall as fast as they could. "Maybe we'll meet in the middle!" said the little young girl, tossing a bit of Greed onto the pile.

Quick as prairie dogs, the little old people set to work again. Soon the pile began to grow higher. The woman with the red hat said, "Well, I've got a few minutes to spare. I could help a little." And she did. Then others came to help, too. And with everyone helping, eventually they made a hole in the wall. And there, on the other side, stood a little young boy and a little young girl. "We've been waiting for you!" they cried. "Come on!"

"I knew we could do it!" shouted the man with the blue hat and the woman with the red hat, both at the same time. "You go on through the wall," said the man to the old people. "We'll just stay here and keep chipping at it," declared the woman, fanning her face with her red hat.

And so the little old woman and the little old man stepped through the wall and walked to the children on the other side of the mountain, carrying stories and songs and dreams.

The End

or maybe—

The Beginning...

Peacing It Together with Today

In the fable, *The Wall*, the little old man and the little old woman take a bag filled with stories, songs, and dreams to children. In Ottawa, Ontario two women became the first in Canada to take stories, songs, and dreams to children in a Peacemobile.[1]

Inspired by an original idea that came from Andi Melham and her family in Atlanta, Georgia, Barbara Kernohan and Wanda White have created a mobile activity centre that helps kids from kindergarten to grade 6 learn about peacemaking–in both official languages. The Peacemobile program offers games and activities:

Peace for Me highlights self-esteem.
Peace for Us is about relationships with family and friends.
Peace for Everyone is about diversity in the world.
Peace for the Planet is about respecting the natural world.

Barbara and Wanda have presented programs that help develop peacemaking skills to campers, kids in parks and schools, and also to youth groups who are interested in the possibilities of peace and teaching peace.

"Peacemobile" Brainstorming

If you were going to help children in kindergarten or grade 1 learn about making peace in the four categories above, what would you do? What stories would you tell? What art activities would you suggest? What games would you play? What songs would you sing?

If you have a chance to work with young children, to baby-sit them or take care of them, how could you *become* a "peacemobile"?

Peacing It Together with Our Faith

> *I therefore, the prisoner in the Lord, beg you to lead a life worthy of the calling to which you have been called, with all humility and gentleness, with patience, bearing with one another in love, making every effort to maintain the unity of the Spirit in the bond of peace.*
> (Ephesians 4:1-3)

Paul writes to the church at Ephesus that Christ makes unity and peace possible and that people must work hard to maintain peace.

[1] For more information on Peacemobile Ottawa Valley, call: 613-355-0488.

A New Day
The Wall

Learn some songs of peace: "Go Now in Peace" and "Dona Nobis Pacem" can both be found in the *Voices United* hymn book (VU 964 and VU 955 respectively). Another version of "Dona Nobis Pacem" (#95) can be found in *Joyful Noise: Songs of Faith and Fun for Children* (Toronto: United Church Publishing House), as well as the old favourite, "I've Got Peace Like a River." (#20)

Crafting Peace: Kites of Peace[2]

Long ago when humans only dreamed of flying, they began to invent kites. When they flew them, people imagined the freedom of looking at the world in a different way–from the sky. They imagined flying out over water, above trees, across boundaries, over walls.

In China where kites are especially loved, children and adults spend days and weeks creating beautiful kites. They paint powerful symbols on their kites, then set them free to dance and soar in the wind. Invite the children to create a peace kite and decorate it with a powerful symbol of peace. The white poppy, the crane, a circle of people around Earth, and a dove are all symbols that people easily recognize.

Kites can be flown as part of the group experience or they can be hung as an artistic symbol of peace in your gathering room, on a door, or anywhere.

What you need
- 6 sheets of newspaper
- masking tape
- paint and a paint brush
- a ball of light string
- ruler and scissors

What you do
1. Tape together 2 sheets of newspaper.
2. Measure 180 mm from each corner of the newspaper, draw lines to connect the points, and cut as illustrated.(1)
3. Tape around the outside of the kite. Tape across the middle of the kite as shown. (2)
4. Use 2 more sheets of newspaper to make a tight roll. Tape it securely. This roll will be one of your "sticks." Repeat this to make the second "stick." (3)
5. Tape the "sticks" in place.(4)
6. Cut 1 length of string 1.5 m. Attach each end of the string to the bot-

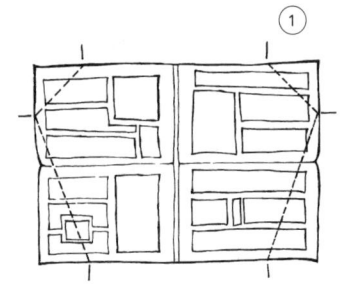

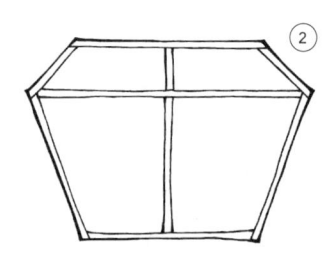

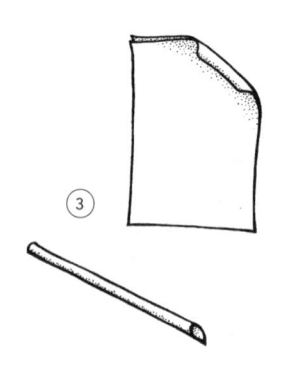

tom corners of the kite. Cut a second 1.5 m. length and attach each end of it to the top corners of the kite. Tie your flying string securely to the centre of this. (5)

7. Add narrow, rainbow-coloured ribbons to the bottom centre of your kite.
8. Paint your peace symbol (e.g. a dove, the peace sign, olive branch, rainbow).
9. Go fly a kite!

[2] The idea for this kite is from Dave who makes them with his Scout troop in England. You can visit his website at www.clem.freeserve.co.uk.

Peace Words (see Reproducible Activity Page, page 62)

Photocopy page 62. Make sufficient copies for the children to have a page each. However, encourage the children to work together in pairs or small groups.

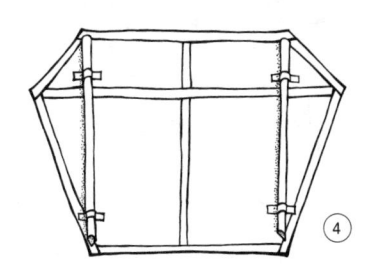

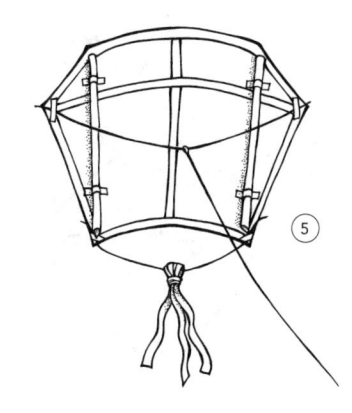

Solution

A New Day
The Wall

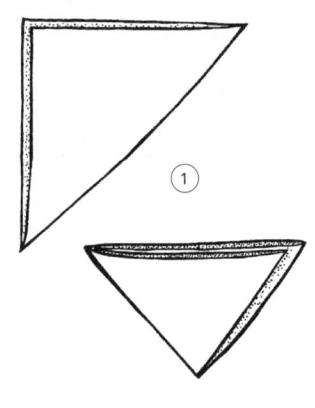

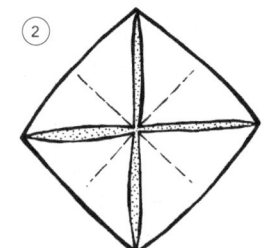

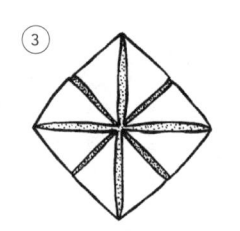

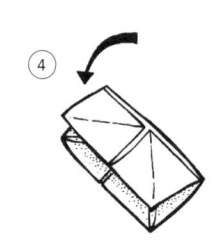

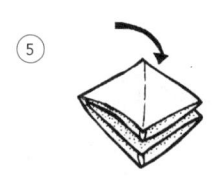

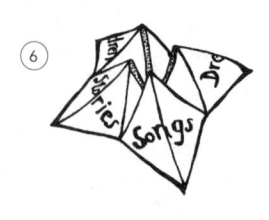

Origami Peacemaker (see Reproducible Activity Page, page 63)

Before the session with the children, practise folding the Origami Peacemaker according to the diagrams at left:

1. Prep the paper by folding the Peacemaker square in half, twice. (1) Reopen.
2. With the blank side facing you, fold the four corners so that they meet in the middle. (2)
3. Keeping the folds made in step 2, flip your Peacemaker and fold the four corners to meet in the middle. (3)
4. Fold in half and then into quarters, pressing the folds firmly. (4) and (5)
5. Unfold the last two folds.
6. Gently ease thumbs and first fingers into the four 'pockets.' (6)

Playing in pairs, one child fits the thumb and first finger of each hand into the four 'pockets.' This child invites his/her partner to select from the words SONGS, STORIES, DREAMS, or CHILDREN. The first child then moves the Peacemaker back and forth according to the number of letters of the word chosen–spelling aloud the letters as s/he does so. Whichever position the Peacemaker is held at on the call of the final letter, the children will see the names of four famous peacemakers. The second child chooses one of the names, and the first child moves the Peacemaker back and forth according to the number by the name. Again, the children will be presented with the names of four peacemakers. The second child chooses one, and the first child lifts the flap to read more about the person selected.

Photocopy page 63. Make sufficient copies so that each child has at least one Origami Peacemaker. Introduce the topic of peacemakers. Invite the children to name any peacemakers they have heard about. You might talk about some of the peacemakers mentioned in the story, "The Wall," and in particular the peacemakers highlighted on the Origami Peacemaker. Encourage the children to name local peacemakers, including friends and family members. Encourage them to name instances of when they too have been peacemakers.

Hand each child a copy of page 63. Point out that the Origami Peacemaker mirrors the story of "The Wall." The dreams, songs, and stories carried by the old man and old woman could not reach the children because of a wall. It takes peacemakers–people of all ages and sizes–to break through the walls that prevent peace. Before they fold the Origami Peacemakers, invite the children to draw a symbol of peace and/or write a message of peace in each of the hearts in the centre of the Peacemakers. (Be prepared to help those who might have some difficulty when following the folding instructions.)

Into the World: Peace Poles

In 1955, 10 years after the horror of World War II, Japanese poet Misahisa Goi wrote a simple prayer: "May peace prevail on Earth." The prayer was written on four sides of a pole, so that the prayer 'went out' in the four directions. Fifty years later, this simple prayer and Misahisa's simple idea has spread around the world. There are now 200,000 peace poles in 180 countries! They can be found in parks, schoolyards, gardens, and town squares. They can be found indoors and out. There is one at the Magnetic North Pole in Canada and another at the Pyramids of El Giza in Egypt. The Dalai Lama, Pope John Paul II, and Mother Teresa have helped to plant peace poles. Your group might like to plant a peace pole too!

Discuss the idea with the group and get appropriate permission before planting a peace pole. Some people create their own peace pole using local wood and writing the prayer in different languages on each side. Other people raise money to buy one or have one made. They are usually about 2.5 metres tall and look a little like tall fence posts. The sides are straight so that the writing shows well. Your group might like to organize a special celebration to commemorate peace and the hope for peace.

Your celebration might include a speech by one of the children, saying why the group thought planting a peace pole was a good idea. Other children might like to share information about peace poles planted in other parts of the world. The celebration might include:

- a poem for peace (e.g. page 60) or readings from different faith traditions
- people reading from the peace pole in another/their own language
- 'planting' other prayers for peace or other peace mementos
- inviting a children's choir and/or musicians to sing
- inviting everyone to sing a song for peace
- sharing stories about peacemakers (e.g. page 61)

A New Day
The Wall

If the Earth

*If the Earth were only
a few feet in diameter, floating a
few feet above a field somewhere,
people would come from everywhere to
marvel at it. People would walk around it,
marvelling at its big pools of water, its little pools
and the water flowing between the pools. People would
marvel at the bumps on it, and the holes in it, and they
would marvel at the very thin layer of gas surrounding it and
the water suspended in the gas. The people would marvel at
all the creatures walking around the surface of the ball, and
at the creatures in the water. The people would declare it
precious because it was the only one, and they would protect
it so that it would not be hurt. The ball would be the
greatest wonder known, and people would come to behold
it, to be healed, to gain knowledge, to know beauty
and to wonder how it could be. People would love
it, and defend it with their lives, because
they would somehow know that their
lives, their own roundness, could be
nothing without it. If the Earth
were only a few feet
in diameter.*

Author unknown

Peacemakers Everywhere

(Encourage children to name local peacemakers, including themselves!)

Shirin Ebadi • Women for Women Afghanistan • One World Child Development Centre • Vision Television • The Raging Grannies • Nigerian Mamas • Change for Children • Children for Peace • Jim Endicott • Code Pink • Youth Hostel Association • Terry Wolfwood • Gerd Weih • Pat Brownlee • Paul Armstrong • Bill Phipps • Ted Reeve • Donna McPhee • Bob Smith • Desmond Tutu • Jesus • Arthur Solomon • Buddha • Mohammed • Ernie Rehger • Eric Tollefson • Bill Vendley • Prince Hassan • Craig Kielburger • Marc Kielburger • Romeo Dallaire • Lloyd Axworthy • Jean Vanier • Voice of Women • Rosemary Brown • Committee Against Racism • Dominique de Villepen • Evelyn Hamdon • Aung San Suu Kyi • Pollution Probe • Kaye MacPherson • Lysistrata Project • 2/15 Project • Pauline Johnson • Barbara Shoomski • Lois Wilson • Jean Tollefson • Elda Thomas • Mary Jo Leddy • Paula Whitlow • Chiefswood • Myra Laramee • The Women in Black • Veterans Against Nuclear Arms • Project Ploughshares • Peace Brigades International • Alternatives to Violence • Doctors without Borders • Janet Campbell • ICCHRLA • ICCA • PEN International • Change for Children • Ecology North • Free the Children • International Children's Villages • Lawyers for Social Responsibility • Madres • YMCA • YWCA • RiverKeepers • Roots and Shoots • Red Cross • Red Crescent • World Conference of Religions for Peace • Plant a Tree in Africa • Middle East Non-Violence and Democracy • Dances of Universal Peace • Arab-Jewish Women's Coalition for Peace • Amnesty International • Canadian University Students Overseas • Neve Shalom/Wahat al Salaam/Oasis of Peace • Canadian International Development Agency • Citizens for Public Justice • Aboriginal Rights Coalition • Fair Trade • Green Peace • Gandhian Society • Habitat for Humanity • Intercultural Grandmothers • Kids for Peace • Committee Against Racism • Parkland Institute • Robert Bateman • Troubadour Centre • United Nations • United Nations International Children's Emergency Fund • Voice of Women • Women of Vision and Action • Edan Thomas • L'Arche • The Women's Journey • Severn Cullis-Suzuki • Mothers of the Disappeared • Poundmaker • Derek Evans • Dalai Lama • Bill Belsey • KAIROS • Nelson Mandela • Andrea Czarnecki • The United Church of Canada • Clowns without Borders…

Peace Words

Find the words:

CARE	FIX	AWE
THROUGH	UNDER	HELP
CREATE	REAL	DREAM
TOGETHER	MAKE	FEEL
ME	HOPE	SANITY
PEACEMAKER	TOOLS	FOOD
READY	TRY	ALL
US	DO	FRIEND
OVER	LOVE	END
PEACE	TRANSFORM	IDEA
GO	IMAGINE	HAPPY

C	A	R	E	M	M	U	I	P	O	L	P
H	O	P	E	P	E	A	C	E	B	O	M
F	O	O	D	R	E	A	M	A	I	V	A
I	M	A	G	I	N	E	W	C	E	E	K
F	R	I	E	N	D	C	R	E	A	T	E
T	H	R	O	U	G	H	N	M	H	R	F
R	E	A	L	V	N	I	A	A	A	I	E
A	L	L	P	D	E	D	U	K	P	U	E
N	P	X	R	E	D	R	E	E	P	Q	L
S	S	Y	R	T	T	A	R	R	Y	L	U
F	I	X	O	O	O	T	V	G	H	W	S
O	D	D	O	T	O	G	E	T	H	E	R
R	E	A	D	Y	L	O	X	C	U	B	F
M	A	C	O	T	S	A	N	I	T	Y	X

A New Day
Reproducible Activity Page — The Wall

Origami Peacemaker

Copy this page and cut along the solid line. Follow folding instructions on page 58.

- 1. Nellie McClung — helped Canadian women get the vote
- 2. Craig Kielburger — founded "Free the Children"
- 3. Rachel Carson — warned about polluting the environment
- 4. Nelson Mandela — opposed racism in South Africa
- 5. Helen Caldicott — works to save children from nuclear poisons
- 6. Jesus — said "Blessed are the peacemakers"
- 7. Rosa Parks — was arrested for refusing to give up her seat on the bus for a white person
- 8. David Swann — takes messages of peace to war areas

Dreams · Songs · Stories · Children

63

Author's Notes

The seed for **"The Other Flood"** came after reading a Jewish tale in the book, *Out of the Ark: Stories from the World's Religions*. On International Women's Day in 1999, Judy Chapman, a Scarboro United Church minister, offered me the privilege of reading "The Other Flood" in place of the sermon. Later, I printed the story as an illustrated booklet.

"Dragons" is the combination of two tales told for hundreds of years in Europe and Britain. I had heard about St. George as a child, but it wasn't until Senator Reverend Lois Wilson published *Mary, Miriam, and Me* that I learned about St. Martha and the dragon. This story has been used for peace education in Calgary at PeaceCamp and Lakeview United Church, used as inspiration for a puppet play at The Museum of the Regiments, and was published by *The United Church Observer* in November, 2003.

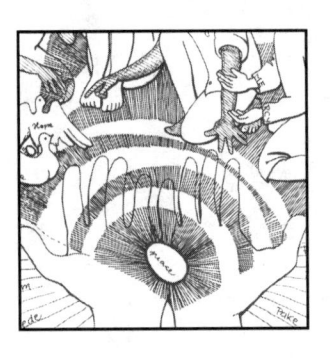

"The Egg" was written as a gift to peacemakers in the Middle East. The seed for this story was a question: What would have happened in the story of Noah if the dove couldn't find a place to land? In 2002 I printed illustrated copies of the story for people in Jerusalem, Ramallah, Tel Aviv, Qalqilya, and other communities, who are working hard to keep the precious egg safe. I dedicated it to Women in Black worldwide. When my friend Karen delivered the story to the office of the Middle East Non-Violence and Democracy in Jerusalem, Lucy said, "Karen, turn and look on the window ledge." There was a dove in her nest, sitting on her eggs!

In March 2003, I read **"The Wall"** at UpRising in Calgary, a political/cultural ideas exchange organized by Symbiosis. I later read it on CJSW, University of Calgary radio, and then printed the story as an illustrated booklet. The seed for this story came after a January 2003 visit to Palestine and Israel. I came home thinking about children who are forced to live behind physical, spiritual, and economic walls there, in Canada, and everywhere. Will adults stop building walls? If children help us, will we have the courage to walk through walls that do exist?

"Enough" was the last story written for this collection. Watching magpies build their amazing nests (with a front and back entrance and a roof), talking with children about the fun of walking outside without boots, and feeling Earth stir from winter filled me with gratitude and wonder even though it was my 55th spring! I worry about Earth, quietly working miracles every single day. I worry that she is suffering because fewer people are connected to the land in a personal way. People are forgetting what they once knew. *When humans remember that there is enough, they are happy. They have courage for hard times. They have love for each other and for the planet. It is enough.*